Awesome After Cancer

A Prescription For Life

DR. TONYA

AWESOME AFTER CANCER
Published by Purposely Created Publishing Group™
Copyright © 2018 Tonya Cole

All rights reserved.

No part of this book may be reproduced, distributed or transmitted in any form by any means, graphic, electronic, or mechanical, including photocopy, recording, taping, or by any information storage or retrieval system, without permission in writing from the publisher, except in the case of reprints in the context of reviews, quotes, or references.

Limit of Liability / Disclaimer of Warranty: While the publisher and author have used their best efforts in preparing this book, they make no representations or warranties with the respect to the accuracy or completeness of the contents of this book and specifically disclaim any implied warranties of fitness for a particular purpose. No warranty may be created or extended by sales representatives or written sales materials. The advice and strategies contained herein may not be suitable for your situation. You should consult with a doctor where appropriate. Neither the publisher nor author shall be liable for any loss or damages including but not limited to special, incidental, consequential or other damages.

DrTonyaMD.com books and products are available through online book retailers. To contact DrTonyaMD.com directly, call our Customer Service Department within the U.S. at 404-855-2223

Printed in the United States of America
ISBN: 978-1-948400-68-8

Special discounts are available on bulk quantity purchases by book clubs, associations and special interest groups. For details email info@DrTonyaMd.com.

For information logon to:
www.DrTonyaMD.com

DEDICATION

To all my #Canterpillars, #Cancerbeauties, and #Cancerbeaus:

I wrote this book especially for you beautiful people. Let me clarify the categories for those who may not be familiar with DrTonyaMD.com and The Beauty of Cancer. A #Canterpillar is a cancer patient who is still getting treatment. #Cancerbeauties are female cancer patients who have completed treatment, who have broken out of their cocoons and transformed into beautiful butterflies, ready to soar. And #Cancerbeaus are the men who have beaten cancer.

I get asked all the time by patients: "What should I be doing, now that I'm done with treatment?" I used to give the textbook answer. Eat right, exercise, you know the drill. But now, this doctor turned #Canterpillar, turned #Cancerbeauty, can give you real-world advice, because I lived it and know what we need. It's not just about keeping the cancer from coming back. It's about living your best life right now. It is about realizing your beauty and loving the skin you are in. It IS possible to live a life that is happier and more fulfilled than you ever dreamed was possible AFTER having cancer.

Are you ready to live such a life? Well, sit back and let me show you how to be awesome after cancer.

TABLE OF CONTENTS

Preface 1

CHAPTER 1:
What Are You, Cancer? 5

CHAPTER 2:
I'm a Survivor 9

CHAPTER 3:
What About Me? 13

CHAPTER 4:
Find Your Joy 17

CHAPTER 5:
Spell It Out 21

CHAPTER 6:
Create Some Space 27

CHAPTER 7:
Push Past Your Fear 31

CHAPTER 8:
Prioritize You 35

CHAPTER 9:
Embrace the New You 39

CHAPTER 10:
Make Life a Party 47

CHAPTER 11:
Discover the Magic 53

CHAPTER 12:
Assess Associations 57

CHAPTER 13:
Stay Connected 61

CHAPTER 14:
Manage Your Mood 67

CHAPTER 15:
Protect Your Body 73

CHAPTER 16:
Snatch Your Sexy Back 77

CHAPTER 17:
Get Fit for Life 83

CHAPTER 18:
Be Fulfilled 89

CHAPTER 19:
From Lack to Luxury 93

CHAPTER 20:
Conclusion 103

Resources 105

Thank You 107

About the Author 111

PREFACE

My courtship with cancer started over twenty years ago as an eager third-year medical student doing a two-week elective course that introduced me to many of the specialty fields of cancer. Six years later I completed my training and became a board-certified radiation oncologist. Over the next two decades, I devoted my life to delivering quality, compassionate care to cancer patients and educating the community on cancer prevention.

Not once in those twenty years did I ever imagine that I would need the same care I've been providing to others. In December of 2014, however, after going in for a routine screening mammogram, my personal cancer journey began.

On a Friday afternoon, while en route to meet a girlfriend for lunch, the nurse called to let me know that "they saw something" on my mammogram and that I needed to come in for additional images. I figured I would go right away, since it would be a quick exam. I wasn't worried, because 95 percent of abnormal mammograms are not cancer. I'd be in and out quickly and off to my lunch date. As I drove to the breast center, my thoughts raced as I wondered if what they saw was "real." I hadn't thought to ask the nurse what they saw; I just assumed it was nothing. I quickly dismissed the thought, reassured myself it was nothing, and went in for my exam. As the technician placed my breast on the cold plate of the mammography unit, I could feel my heart race in anticipation of the test. I held my breath and heard the machine beep as it took the image. My heart sank to the pit of my stomach as the image of my breast appeared on the screen across the room—with an irregular white mass. It was "real." It was an image I have seen many times before. It was the textbook picture of what cancer looks like on a mammogram.

All I could think was that my daughters were only two years old and they needed me. My quick in-and-out exam turned into three hours of additional imaging and a biopsy. My surgeon colleague told me not to freak out as the long needle she used to do the biopsy pierced through my skin. I heard what sounded like a vacuum suction as the needle withdrew with the sample, leaving a burning sensation in my right breast. She had arranged for the pathologist to stay late and examine the tissue so

I could get an answer right away. I told her to send them home. I could wait until Monday. I already knew what it was and I didn't want an official confirmation of that to ruin my weekend.

On Monday, she told me what I already knew: I had cancer. I was diagnosed with a stage II triple negative breast cancer. Over the next year, I would have both of my breasts removed and reconstructed. I would endure six months of aggressive chemotherapy and two months of radiation treatments. Because of a cancerous gene I carry, I had to have my uterus and ovaries removed as well.

Being self-employed and unable to work, I accumulated over $175,000 of debt and nearly went bankrupt. Just as I was finishing treatment, a hit-and-run driver caused my car to hydroplane and slam into the concrete barrier at the side of the road, completely destroying my car. In one year, I lost my womanhood, my confidence, my self-esteem, and my vehicle. I found thirty extra pounds, developed swelling in my right arm from lymphedema, and sank into a deep depression requiring medication. For the first time in my life I really understood what my patients were going through.

How do you bounce back after such a huge setback?

I was in a unique situation. I was a cancer doctor who had cancer. And being a doctor didn't shield me from any of the harsh realities that can occur along the cancer journey. For the first time in my life, I had come face to face with my own mortality.

Many of you already know that periods of great suffering can bring about positive change. To be honest, I didn't realize that cancer would be the life experience to change me. Treating cancer patients has always given me great satisfaction, but I never felt that my touch went any further than the particular family that was touched by my expertise. I realize now that I can touch people far beyond the four walls of my office and help people everywhere be their best self and live their best lives after adversity.

I fought back from all the problems and completely changed my life. I want to help other survivors do the same. Having cancer has completely changed the way I practice medicine. I now know cancer patients need much more than just a cure for their cancer; they need help regaining what cancer took from them and help living a normal life after cancer as well. This book shows you how I became awesome after cancer—and I want you to be awesome too.

Chapter 1

WHAT ARE YOU, CANCER?

Cancer affects all of us, whether you're a daughter, mother, sister, friend, coworker, doctor, patient.

—Jennifer Aniston

Cancer, stated simply, is an over-growth of cells in the body that have mutated and no longer respond to the checks and balances that the body has to control its growth. A mutation is an alteration in DNA (deoxyribonucleic acid), the molecules that contain the instructions an organism needs to develop, live, and reproduce. Once a normal cell has mutated into a cancerous cell, it can grow out of control and invade other tissues, robbing them of the nutrients and oxygen they need to grow and function normally. These invaded tissues then malfunction or die and cause a whole host of problems in the body that, if left untreated, can ultimately lead to death.

The vast majority of cancers are caused by environmental exposures. These exposures include poor diet, tobacco, alcohol, radiation, infectious agents, and substances in the air, water, and soil. Only 10 percent of cancers are inherited from genes passed down from our parents.

Cancer can develop in any cell of the body. Although cancers develop in much the same way in each cell, each cancer is different. Cancer is not just one disease, it is many diseases. Some cancers grow very fast and other cancers grow very slowly. Some cancers have a tendency to spread quickly to other parts of the body, while other cancers stay and grow in the area of origin.

The treatment of cancer varies depending on the cell of origin, the location in the body where the cancer is located, and the tumor biology. Treatment of cancer is divided into two main categories: systemic treatment and local treatment. Local treatments include things such as surgery and radiation. Systemic treatments are things like chemotherapy, hormone therapy, immunotherapy, and biologic agents.

Your doctor has outlined or will outline the best treatment plan for you based on your specific type of cancer. Don't hesitate to ask questions. Make sure you understand the anticipated short-term and long-term side effects of each treatment. Some of the long-term side effects related to your treatment will play a huge role in determining the quality of your life in the future.

Chapter 2

I'M A SURVIVOR

*You need to spend time crawling alone
through shadows to truly appreciate what it is
to stand in the sun.*

—Shaun Hick

No one plans to get cancer. No one wishes for cancer. You don't go shopping for cancer and you can't catch cancer from someone else. But the American Cancer Society statistics show that almost 1.7 million people get diagnosed with cancer in the United States every year. That is about 4,600 new cases every day. When people hear the word *cancer*, they immediately think about death and dying. Everyone has a story about a friend or loved one who was diagnosed with cancer and ultimately died of the disease. But cancer is not the number one cause of death in the United States. Cardiovascular diseases such as heart disease and stroke claim more lives each year than all forms of cancer combined.

In the twenty years that I have been treating patients with cancer, the death rates from many forms of cancer have dropped significantly. This is because there have been tremendous advances in cancer treatment over the years. Cancer screening programs, community education, and early detection techniques allow for cancer to be diagnosed at earlier stages. There has also been improved access to care for people living in rural areas and funding to help uninsured and underinsured people get the care they need.

More than 60 percent of cancers diagnosed in the United States are curable. Cancer is not a death sentence for most people. The American Cancer Society statistics show that there are over 15.5 million cancer survivors in the US today. And that number is expected to increase to 20 million over the next decade. A cancer survivor is defined as anyone who is living with a history of having cancer. They are split about equally between men and women. Fifty percent of them are under the age of seventy.

Cancer survivors represent a diverse group of individuals in varying phases of treatment and survivorship. The American Cancer Society shows that survivors encompass a wide range of trajectories and experiences that include:

- Those who live cancer-free after treatment for the remainder of their lives.

- Those who live cancer-free after treatment for many years, but experience one or more complications of treatment.

- Those who live cancer-free after treatment for many years, but die after a late recurrence.

- Those who live cancer-free after the first cancer is treated, but develop a second cancer.

- Those who live with intermittent periods of active disease requiring treatment.

- Those who live with cancer continuously, with or without treatment, without having a disease-free period.

For cancer survivors, the end of the initial treatment is just the beginning of a life of survivorship filled with many possible twists and turns. Every survivor has a unique journey. No matter where you are along your journey, you can create a life that you never imagined. The chapters that follow will show you how to live awesome as you navigate through the twists and turns that occur along your cancer journey.

Chapter 3

WHAT ABOUT ME?

Life is a terminal condition. We're all going to die. Cancer patients just have more information, but we all, in some ways, wait for permission to live.

—**Kris Carr**

I know some of you are thinking to yourself: how can I be awesome after cancer? I still have cancer and will always have cancer because my cancer cannot be cured. Newsflash: You can still be awesome, even if you are living with metastatic disease (a cancer that returns or that has spread to another part of the body) and even if you've been told that your disease is terminal.

Because the statistics of people who were diagnosed with cancer that has returned are not kept, it is hard to quantify the number of people living with metastatic disease. But realize you are not alone. In a recent study done by Angela Mariotto, PhD, in conjunction with the National Cancer Institute and the Metastatic Breast Cancer Alliance, the number of women living with metastatic disease is rising. They estimate that as of January 1, 2017, there are over 150,000 women in the United States living with metastatic breast cancer. Of these women, three out of four of them had originally been diagnosed with an earlier-stage disease. Based on their calculations, they expect that number to increase by 31 percent from 2010 to 2020. And remember, this study is just looking at breast cancer patients. If we could add the number of people with other types of cancer, those numbers would be astounding.

Because of advances in treatment and our aging population, people are living much longer with disease. Cancer is quickly becoming a chronic disease, just like diabetes or hypertension. Many people live for years or even decades with metastatic disease. Some people have long periods of stable disease, and other people are continuously on some type of therapy. Life doesn't stop just because you have metastatic disease.

Being awesome after cancer is not just about curing the cancer and living free of disease.

You just have to decide what *awesome* is for you. You can still have a life that is rich with purpose, meaningful work or volunteer activities, and close relationships. It is never too late to become the person you have always wanted to be and have the things you have always wanted to have. Having metastatic disease just gives you urgency like no other to evoke the change you want and need in your life. You will still be scared at times—and that is okay. Stephen Covey, author of the book *The 7 Habits of Highly Effective People*, said that "courage is not the absence of fear but the awareness there is something more important." Beating cancer and living an awesome life is that thing that is more important.

As American sportscaster and ESPN anchor Stuart Scott put it in his 2014 ESPY speech, "you beat cancer by how you live, why you live, and in the manner in which you live." So why not live it awesome?

Chapter 4

FIND YOUR JOY

*Find a place inside where there's joy,
and the joy will burn out the pain.*

—Joseph Campbell

So even though it wasn't planned and you didn't wish for it, you got it. You were diagnosed with cancer. You probably don't even remember the initial conversation with your doctor when you were told the news. Without knowing it, your mind took over. Your thoughts drifted and you saw your life pass before your eyes. You began to take an inventory of how prepared your family would be for the possibility of you not being there. You thought about work or school. Will I lose my job? How will I pay my bills? Will I get sick? Will I lose my hair? Who will take care of my kids? These are common questions that most survivors think about.

Suddenly, just like that, life, *your* life, changed. Your schedule is now filled with doctor's appointments, tests, and procedures. The days when you feel bad outnumber the days when you feel good. You feel like you are always at the doctor's office. It seems as if cancer is consuming your life. It is easy to start feeling depressed during this time. It seems as if you have no control over what is going on. Cancer is dictating your coming and going, your appetite, your energy, and even your mood.

Even with all of this going on, it is possible to live awesome in the midst of it. You just have to be intentional about it. You must remember that nothing, no disease, no side effect, no person, can take away your joy without your permission. YOU are in control. You have the freedom to choose to have joy or to be sad.

While getting my treatment, I chose to be sad, but I tried to make everyone think I was happy. I really tried to be happy. I did things to make myself look happy, too. I kept a smile on my face. I dressed up and wore nice hats, scarves, and wigs. Trying to be happy, though, was just a mask for my sadness. What I really needed was joy.

Some of you are thinking: aren't joy and happiness the same thing? No, they are very different. Happiness is a temporary state. It only satisfies for a short time. We all think, "If I didn't have cancer, I'd be happy. If I could just grow my hair back, get my sense of taste back, lose some weight, and get this guy or that girl, I would be happy." Many times we get the things that we wish for and still find ourselves unhappy. That's because what we really need is to find joy.

Happiness is a feeling that you have on the outside. It is affected by what is happening in your life at the time. Any person, thing, or event can make you happy or take away your happiness.

Joy is a feeling you have on the inside. It is unaffected by anything going on in your life. It is a stronger, deeper feeling than happiness. Joy develops as a result of a personal spiritual connection with God or another person. It is an internal emotion that is deep and long-lasting, like the feeling you get when you marry your one true love, or when you first look at the baby you carried inside you for nine months. Nothing can touch your joy.

Part of being awesome after cancer is choosing to find your joy. That may mean creating a spiritual connection with God or the universe, or creating or deepening a relationship with another person, such as a spouse, sibling, or close friend.

Chapter 5

SPELL IT OUT

Understand that the right to choose your own path is a sacred privilege. Use it. Dwell in possibility.

—**Oprah Winfrey**

So, when I decided that I wanted to live awesome after cancer, I had to figure out what *awesome* was for me. Sadly, I didn't get this epiphany until I was completely done with my treatment. I knew that my life before cancer was not awesome. I was depressed. I was tired. I was overweight. I didn't feel attractive. I was frustrated in my job. I was broke. I knew there was something else I needed to be doing. Something needed to change. I wanted something different. I needed to recreate myself. I needed a rebirth, a do-over, if you will.

In order to change your life, YOU have to change. True change happens from the inside out. To recreate yourself, you have to change who and what you are on the inside so the results can be seen on the outside. You may have to become unrecognizable to those who know you. The beauty of cancer is that the cancer and its treatment change your body from the inside out already. Those changes happen at a cellular level. It affects your DNA, the very essence of who you are on the inside. You may have changes in your bodily appearance or function as well: a new voice, different hair, scars, or skin changes. You may have had organs or limbs removed or altered. Your body is different after cancer treatment, and we have to acclimate ourselves to this new normal.

So while you are adjusting to a new body, why not use this as an opportunity to adjust your mind? Decide what things need to change in regards to your health and fitness. Do you have some relationships you need to repair or strengthen? Are there some personal goals that you have been putting on the backburner? This is a great time to reevaluate your career and your finances. Are there some hobbies and leisure activities that you have been putting off because you have been too busy? What contribution do you want to make to your community or the world?

I know dying is the last thing you want to think about right now, but cancer makes you realize that your life has a definite end—and that that end may come sooner than you expected. If you died today and you were able to watch your own funeral, what would people say about you? Think about what a close friend would say, or a coworker, or a person from your church or community. How would your family members describe you? Do you think they would have nice things to say about you? Did you make a positive impact on or in their lives? Are you the person that you want to be? There is no time to waste. Every minute of every hour of going forward should be spent creating the life you want and becoming the person you always wanted to be.

The extra downtime that cancer treatment creates is an excellent time to really sit and figure out what you want. Many of us are so busy being busy, we don't ever get around to doing the things that are really important to us. We sleepwalk through life. Cancer is a wakeup call. It is the alarm clock that we didn't know we needed.

Use a journal to write down all the things you want to change about your life and put them in order of importance. These are your goals. Now you have a visual representation of what you need to prioritize going forward. Your goals allow you a mechanism to evaluate how successful you are at creating the change you want for your life.

To be effective, your goals must be specific. They must clearly state the objective that is wanted, with details. The goal must be measurable. It should include specific numbers, amounts, and dates. Goals should have a deadline. If you don't give yourself a "when by" date, then there is no urgency set around getting the task completed. You and anyone else should be able to determine whether or not you have achieved your goal. You should review your goals several times every day. You may have some goals that seem impossible to accomplish, but that is okay. Once your mind knows what those goals are, it will work hard to make those things come to pass.

Once you have your goals listed, break each goal down into smaller tasks that are easy to complete. As you complete each task, cross it off your list. Each time you cross something off your list, you will feel a sense of accomplishment and stay motivated to keep working toward your goal.

I know some of you are thinking: what if I create these grand plans and goals for my life and then my cancer comes back? What then? Well, you cannot live your life in fear of things that you have no control over. You could get hit by a car, have a stroke, or have any catastrophic event happen that could derail even the most well-thought-out plans. But you must live inside a space of possibility, of "I know that anything is possible," despite what may happen. You must be fluid and flexible and able to redirect or recraft your goals to fit the new situation. You must not be married to the method by which you thought you could achieve the goal. The best-made plans sometimes need to be redrafted. Just remember, no matter what happens in your life, you can still be awesome. You can still create a life of pleasure and purpose.

Chapter 6

CREATE SOME SPACE

When we clear the physical clutter from our lives, we literally make way for inspiration and "good, orderly direction" to enter.

—Julia Cameron

In order to be awesome, you have to create space for the awesomeness to thrive and grow. This means you must clear away the clutter in your life that is distracting you from your goals. We all have things in our lives that we tolerate. Things that bother us, that we wish were different. Each one of these things takes up critical space in our brains that could be devoted to something else. And if you have chemo brain, like I do, you need all of your available neurons that have not been affected by cancer treatment working on important stuff.

What is chemo brain, you ask? It is a group of mental issues that can be described as a change in mental clarity. It is a real phenomenon. It can occur during treatment or even after treatment has been completed. Patients can have a variety of symptoms, including memory lapses, problems finding the words they need to finish a sentence, problems concentrating, difficulty remembering details like places and people's names, and having to take longer to complete tasks. You can't control your chemo brain symptoms, but you can control your life clutter.

What are you tolerating? What clutter is causing you unnecessary brain chatter and pulling energy and resources from the goals you want to achieve? This clutter can take the form of many things:

- Stacks of unopened mail
- A disorganized desk
- Closets so packed that you cannot get anything in or out of them
- A pantry full of expired or half-eaten, stale food

- A stain on the carpet that you keep walking over
- A garage full of unusable junk
- Incomplete home projects
- Unorganized business or tax records
- Bags of baby items that need to be donated or sold
- Half-written books

The more clutter you have in your life, the more discouraged you become about being able to handle bigger tasks in your life. You think to yourself, "If I can't control the clutter on my desk, how can I start my own business?"

Make a list of those things that you are tolerating. Organize them in order of how much they are bothering you. Set a goal to complete one of these things every month. As you complete things on your list, you will feel happier and more accomplished. If you have larger tasks on your list, don't feel like you have to complete the project in one sitting. You may have to do a little every day or every week until you get it done. Taking care of these little things will make your life easier and give you more confidence in moving forward with the projects you need to do to achieve the goals and dreams you have set for yourself. It will free your mind from focusing on the things that hold you back.

Now, once you cross something off your list, make sure you create a new habit or routine to ensure that that item does not reappear on your list again. Keep a running list, so that you can handle them quickly and not let them pile up.

Chapter 7

PUSH PAST YOUR FEAR

The only thing we have to fear is fear itself.
—Franklin D. Roosevelt

Fear is a common theme that surfaces at multiple times during the journey of a cancer patient. During treatment, you worry about getting sick or dying from treatment. After treatment, you worry about the cancer coming back. Some patients become so worried that they stop coming to the doctor because it causes too much anxiety for them. It's impossible to completely dismiss the negative thoughts, but the goal is to not let them control you. Fear can be a powerful emotion and can cause you to make poor decisions that could negatively impact your health. I have met patients that are more afraid of the cancer treatment than they are of dying from the cancer. I know, it makes no sense, but fear can make the irrational seem rational. How do you push past the fear? Here are five ways that can help:

1. Acknowledge the fear, but move forward in spite of it. Talk with your doctor about what specifically frightens you. If they know what you are uncomfortable or uncertain about, they can give you information that can alleviate your concern.

2. Get more information. The more information you have, the more comfortable you feel. When you don't have all of the information, you make up stories to fill in the gaps in what you know. Those stories you tell yourself may be completely false and take your mind down a path of no return. Make sure the information you get is coming from a credible source. If it is medical information, get the answers you need from a doctor or nurse who is familiar with your case. Don't compare your cancer journey to someone else's. No two cancer journeys are the same. Just because someone else had a poor outcome or specific side effect, doesn't mean that you will too.

3. Live in the moment. Fear arises when you think about the future or dwell on something that happened in the past. When you focus on what is happening right now, in the present moment, there is nothing to fear.

4. Express gratitude. When you think about what you are grateful for, fear naturally dissipates.

5. Think positive. Stay away from negativity. Don't listen to stories that well-meaning friends or family may share with you about another survivor's bad outcome. Don't fill your mind with negative news media stories. I personally made a conscious decision to not watch the news when I was early on in my journey. Even though the stories may not be cancer related, they can still clutter your fragile unconscious mind with negativity that your mind may not process well during an already stressful time.

Don't let fear get the best of you. You can't get to your awesome if fear has you stuck, unable to move forward. To get to awesome, you will need to get out of your comfort zone and do something different.

Chapter 8

PRIORITIZE YOU

Self-care is never a selfish act—it is simply good stewardship of the only gift I have, the gift I was put on earth to offer to others.

—Parker Palmer

You've been through a lot, so now it's time to treat yourself. Make yourself your first priority. Put your self first. If your hair is still growing back, this may be the time to invest in a new wig. Let the wig you have been wearing for a year go and try a new look. If you can, get your nails done. Not having to look at the discoloration on your fingernails and toenails will do wonders for your mind.

Every woman should be professionally styled after completing treatment. If you can't get or afford a stylist, then a good personal shopper can do the same thing. They will help you find clothing that can accentuate your new shape and camouflage any problem areas, as well as make sure your prosthetics, if you now have them, are being worn correctly. You may need new clothing to fit your new size and shape. This is a great time to splurge and update your wardrobe or repurpose things you already own.

Get a set of glamour shots done. Glamour shots make us feel attractive and prestigious. Have someone do your hair and makeup and pick clothing for you. This will allow you to see yourself in a different light. You don't need to hire a fancy, expensive photographer. Good quality, inexpensive photo shoots can be done at local department stores. The cameras on many mobile phones take high-quality photographs. A good friend or colleague may be able to shoot pictures for you as well.

Taking care of yourself includes scheduling time for things, like getting a regular manicure, pedicure, massage, or facial. It also includes things like vacations and leisure activities. If you have vacation time at work, take it. If you're self-employed, schedule in leisure time. And when you're on vacation, leave work at work. We shouldn't reserve activities like these for special occasions. These activities should become a regular part of our schedules. Self-care is important in maintaining our confidence and relieving stress and anxiety.

You must minimize the amount of stress in your life. You can't be awesome if you're always stressed out. There are several ways to minimize stress; many of them include ways to stay organized and manage your time. Eliminate or minimize contact with people who create stress and chaos in your life. Say no to those activities and events that are not moving you toward your goal so that you can say yes to you.

Make sure you're getting enough sleep. Most adults need seven to nine hours, although some people may only need as few as six hours or as many as ten hours of sleep each day. Sleep plays a very important role in regulating the immune system of the body. The immune system is your body's defense system for fighting infections such as cold or flu and for fighting cancer. Sleep deprivation has been associated with weight gain and a decreased ability to lose weight. If you are taking medications such as aromatase inhibitors, like exemestane or letrozole, or steroids that have weight gain as a side effect, it is important that you don't enhance those effects by not getting enough sleep. Sleep deprivation has also been shown to increase rates of depression and increase inflammation in the body. Inflammation has been linked to heart disease, stroke, diabetes, and arthritis. Getting enough sleep has been shown to improve your concentration and memory, spur creativity, and has even been shown to enhance your athletic performance. This is important as you begin your return to physical activity. If you have sleep disorders, such as sleep apnea or trouble falling asleep and staying asleep, it is important that you have those conditions treated. If you snore loudly or have periods of time when you stop breathing during the night, it is likely that you suffer from sleep apnea. Getting those conditions treated not only improves your sleep quality, it can also improve your blood pressure and help you live longer. Talk with your healthcare provider about ways to treat these conditions.

Chapter 9

EMBRACE THE NEW YOU

*God grant me the serenity to accept the things
I cannot change, the courage to change the things
I can, and the wisdom to know the difference.*

—**Reinhold Niebuhr**

Cancer treatment changes you. You are the not the same person now that you were before you were diagnosed. Your body has gone through both physical and emotional changes. Now is the time to rediscover the beauty you have always had.

Your body is different in so many ways. You now have a scar that is unique to you. Your scar may have come from surgery, radiation skin changes and discolorations, or chemotherapy. No one else has the exact same scar in the same position that has healed the same way as your scar. Some of you have one scar. Some of you have several scars. I call them beauty marks. They are part of you, just like the birthmarks we are born with. There is nothing we can do about them. We can't change them, and so we have to accept them as part of our new bodies.

Our bodies are now shaped differently. One or both breasts may be gone, smaller, larger, harder, higher, or lower than they were before. Our stomachs, butts, or thighs may be flatter or fatter. One arm and/or hand may be larger. You may have lost weight or gained weight. No matter what is different about your new body, though, remember that it is your body and it is beautiful. And, just like the body we had before, we have to decide to love and accept it the way it is. We are perfectly imperfect.

If you received chemotherapy, your hair may have fallen out. Did it come back a different texture or color? Embrace the new look. Sometimes the hair may not grow back at all, or it may come in very thin. If this is you, consider wearing it bald or cut very short. Many women can rock that style and look incredible. If this is out of your comfort zone, then consider getting a custom hairpiece made. It will be worth the financial investment, since this is no longer a temporary condition and it now needs a more permanent solution. Consult with a hair loss professional to find the right solution for your individual situation.

Now, don't get me wrong. Even though I want you to embrace the new you, there are some things that can be done to change what makes you unhappy about your new body. Just remember to appreciate the body you have right now as you make the changes you desire. Wigs and hairpieces can solve hair issues. You can use skin creams to lighten or soften discolored skin. Plastic surgeons may be able to help adjust some surgical scars. You can lose or gain weight. It is important to remember, though, that your body may still not look or feel the same as it did before your cancer treatment. You are still going to have to accept the new you. But think of the new you as a newer, better version of your former self. The sooner you do it, the better you will feel about yourself and the faster you will build your confidence and self-esteem.

It's easy to embrace the new you when you put your best foot forward. You should always look your best. Aim to be well-groomed at all times. Your clothes, hair, and makeup should be done. Don't walk out the door looking less than your best. When you look good, you feel good. There is a different aura that you have when you KNOW you look good. Even if you are not going anywhere, spruce yourself up. You have spent many months during treatment off work, not going out socially, and not really having anything to dress up for. You may have forgotten what it feels like to look good and feel attractive. When people know you have been treated for cancer, they expect you to look sick. But, I tell you, it's the best feeling in the world to get a compliment on your looks after everything you've been through. Each compliment reinforces the love that you have for the new you.

At the end of the day, you need to feel good about the way you look. If you are in a hurry, here is a short cut: We all have that one outfit, piece of jewelry, scarf, hat, or pair of shoes that ALWAYS gets us a compliment. Now is the time to wear it. You know someone's going to compliment you. That compliment will take you to your happy place, boost your self-esteem and confidence, and make you feel good about the new you.

AFFIRMATIONS

Affirmations are a great way to build your confidence. An affirmation is a positive declaration, statement, or phrase that you repeat to yourself that describes what you want to have, experience, or be. You describe what you want as if it has already been completed. This technique fills your subconscious mind with the new thoughts and images of the way you want to be. Keep these things in mind when composing your affirmations:

- **Effective affirmations should be positive.** They should always focus on the things you want rather than the things you want to avoid.

- **They should begin with the words I AM.** Your brain interprets these two words as a command, so the brain begins to work to try and make what you want happen for you.

- **Affirmations should be written in the present tense.** Write as if you're experiencing what you want right now.

- **They should be brief.** Keeping them short makes them easy to remember.

- **They should be specific.** Include details. Your brain cannot take action on a command that is not clear.

- **Affirmations should include one dynamic-feeling word.** It should evoke emotion, feeling, or passion.

> **They should be created for yourself, not for other people.** They should be written in your own words and use phrases that you commonly use and can relate to.

A couple examples of some effective affirmations are: "I am brilliant beyond measure, influential, and strong." And, "I am agile and great at 148 pounds."

One of the most effective exercises I did using affirmations was a group training exercise called earth angels. During the exercise, we were put into groups of four people. Each of us was asked to create an affirmation surrounding a limiting belief that we were struggling with. When it was my turn, I stated my affirmation for the rest of the group to hear: "I am brilliant beyond measure, influential, and strong." The other three members of the group then repeated the affirmation back to me: "You are brilliant beyond measure, influential, and strong." We went back and forth, with me saying the affirmation and then my group members repeating the affirmation back to me, for several minutes. At first, it felt weird and a little uncomfortable, saying the affirmation. But as the minutes passed, I became more and more confident in my new belief. By the end of the exercise, I was able to boldly yell to everyone what has always been true, but what I now believed. "I am brilliant beyond measure, influential, and strong." That one exercise removed a big limitation that had been holding me back for so many years.

Affirmations work. But they must be properly written and used in the right way to make the changes you're seeking. You must repeat affirmations regularly and get them into your subconscious. You can write them on index cards and read them to yourself every morning when you get up and every night before you go to bed. You can record yourself on your mobile phone saying your affirmations and play them back to yourself during your downtime. Better yet, you can use your mobile phone to videotape yourself speaking the affirmations and watch it over and over. Either of these last two ways will be extremely effective because you will hear your affirmations spoken to you in your own voice. Whichever way you choose to use them, remember: the key to success for affirmations is repetition, repetition, repetition.

Chapter 10

MAKE LIFE A PARTY

The more you praise and celebrate your life, the more there is in life to celebrate.

—**Oprah Winfrey**

The cancer treatment journey can be a long, difficult road, full of twists and turns and unexpected setbacks. As survivors, we constantly find ourselves thinking about some time far off in the future, when all treatment has been completed and this whole process is but a blur in our memory, never to be thought of again. Thinking in this way can lead to depression, anxiety, or fear. This can cause us to be less resolute in getting the life-saving treatment we need.

So what do you do to stay upbeat and keep yourself in the game so you can win the biggest fight of your life? You celebrate. Celebrate every day. You must choose to celebrate something every day. You can celebrate something simple, such as the peach fuzz you see growing on your scalp after chemotherapy. Or you can celebrate waking up with a little more energy today than you had the day before. It is vitally important that you celebrate the small victories and accomplishments that are made along the treatment journey. These "parties" make the journey seem easier and more tolerable. You should not wait until you complete all of your chemotherapy to celebrate. Celebrate after each cycle. Have an "I lost my hair" party. Celebrate getting your radiation tattoos. Celebrate after completing each week of radiation. Celebrate recovering from surgery. Anything that gets you closer to your healing should be celebrated.

Don't wait for other people to celebrate for you or even with you. Celebrate yourself. And if need be, celebrate by yourself! I sure did. The celebrations don't have to be grand. A simple journal entry with a special picture or quote can suffice. Perhaps take a relaxing bath or read a new book. Treat yourself to your favorite food or even splurge and purchase a small gift for yourself. These small celebrations go a long way in helping you stay encouraged and engaged until you get to the big victory.

Now, when you get to the BIG victory, you can take the celebration up a notch, because you finally did it! You finished your cancer treatment. You are basking in the light at the end of the tunnel. This is a very important milestone that deserves special recognition. You have completed what may prove to be the hardest thing you will ever have to do in life. Although you may feel beat up by the treatment and the lingering fatigue, the aches and pains that are constant reminders of what was, you must be determined to look ahead. Part of rediscovering your beauty is to control the things you can control and to accentuate the positive things.

I love to travel, so, when I completed my treatment, I planned a trip to Cancun, Mexico. I planned it in conjunction with my best friend's wedding. Although money was tight, I decided to stay for a full week. I deserved it. I stayed in a different resort from the wedding party. It was a AAA, five-diamond rated, all-inclusive resort on the beach. I had five whole days, all by myself.

When I arrived, a private shuttle took me to the hotel. The lobby was like nothing I had ever seen before. It was an open air lobby, with lush green plants, waterfalls, and ponds teeming with live fish. I was greeted with a chilled glass of champagne and a cool towel to wipe the beads of sweat from my brow. After checking in, I was driven on a golf cart for what seemed like a mile, through lush gardens with beautiful, bright-colored tropical flowers and pretty birds. When the bellman opened the door, I was speechless at how opulent the rooms were. My suite overlooked the tropical gardens. I had my own personal swimming pool off my terrace. The view of the ocean waves washing ashore on the pristine white sand beach was breathtaking. The other pools on the property were expansive and the property was beautifully landscaped and meticulously maintained. I had never experienced this level of luxury before in my life.

I treated myself to a full body massage and swam in the hydrotherapy pools. I ate foods from many different cultures. I used the relaxing time to reflect and meditate. It was one of the best vacations that I ever experienced. After a full year of doctor appointments, treatments, and surgeries, I couldn't think of a better way to celebrate.

Make sure you do something to celebrate. Have a nice picture taken of you or indulge in a favorite meal or dessert. Get a massage or facial, take a trip, or treat yourself to a new piece of clothing or jewelry. Have a get-together with friends or family or others survivors. It doesn't matter what it is, just acknowledge this milestone in a special way. Even if you completed your treatment a long time ago, it is never too late to celebrate. Celebrate each new year of life you have after cancer just like you celebrate each new year of life after your birth on this earth.

The phrase "party all the time" takes on new meaning when you are a cancer survivor.

Chapter 11

DISCOVER THE MAGIC

Acknowledging the good that is already in your life is the foundation for all abundance.

—Eckhart Tolle

While I going through treatment for my breast cancer, I forgot to say thank you. I know you are wondering, "thank you? Thank you for what?" I forgot to thank God for giving me something like cancer, something that caused me to pause long enough to see that my life was headed in the wrong direction. I was unhappy. I was on autopilot. I would wake in the morning, get dressed, and go to work. I would then pick up the kids on the way home, feed them, and get them to bed, only to do it all again the next day. My husband and I functioned like roommates. Two ships that passed in the night. Both of us were focused on our careers, never making time for family. I was so busy being busy that I didn't even realize my misery.

Cancer interrupted my schedule. It made me think about something different.

Yes, I thought about how horrible cancer was. I complained about the pain, the weight gain, the nausea, feeling tired, the high cost of treatment, missing work, and mounting bills. I felt sorry for myself and got really depressed. While deep in depression, though, I discovered the power of gratitude. Gratitude means being thankful or showing appreciation for something. Gratitude is an amazing thing. So much so that entire books have been written on the subject.

By the end of my treatment, I was very angry with my husband because I felt he wasn't as supportive of me during my illness as I thought he should have been. I wanted him to adjust his work schedule so that he could be home with me on the days I was really sick from the chemotherapy. He would arrange for other people to be home with me and help out with the kids, but he wasn't there. The only adjustments I saw him make to his schedule were to attend some out-of-town events for family or close friends. One night, I sat in bed, boiling with rage, making a mental list of all the things my husband didn't do for me while I was going through my cancer treatment. I didn't want to be in a relationship with someone who I felt didn't take his marriage vows seriously. I vowed to be there through the good and the bad, in sickness and in health. I thought he had too. I was sick, for Christ's sake! Where was he? I wanted a divorce, immediately.

In the midst of my rage, though, I remembered watching a segment on the Oprah show on the topic of gratitude. She spoke of how we should be grateful for the things we do have instead of focusing on what we don't have. She said if you focus on what is good, you will start to feel more joy. Since I definitely needed more joy, my thoughts shifted from thinking about what was bad about my husband to what was good about him. I bought a blank greeting card with the words "thank you" on the front and filled every inch of space with expressions of gratitude, telling my husband what I was thankful for about him. By the time I finished writing on the card, my rage had completely dissipated. I was at peace.

Author Melody Beattie, in her book *The Language of Letting Go*, has this meditation on gratitude:

> Gratitude unlocks the fullness of life. It turns what we have into enough, and more. It turns denial into acceptance, chaos to order, confusion to clarity. It can turn a meal into a feast, a house into a home, a stranger into a friend . . . Gratitude makes sense of our past, brings peace for today, and creates a vision for tomorrow.

Magically, life is so much better when you are giving thanks for everything.

Chapter 12

ASSESS ASSOCIATIONS

Let us be grateful to the people who make us happy; they are the charming gardeners who make our souls blossom.

—Marcel Proust

Going to cancer treatment really gives you a great opportunity to evaluate your relationships with the people in your life. You become aware of which relationships you've been neglecting and which relationships you need to nurture or repair. You find out which people in your life you can count on and what people are there merely to see what they can get from you. You can separate the givers from the takers.

Make a list and decide which relationships you want to water and grow and which ones need to be pruned or cut away. Relationships that cause you anxiety, create chaos, or are unsupportive, negative, and needy need to be severely restricted or eliminated entirely.

Is there someone you have wanted to spend more time with or reconnect with? Do you need to check in on someone to see how he or she is doing? Now you have the time to reestablish those relationships and spend quality time with those who you have been neglecting.

You may need to meet new people and surround yourself with people who are already doing what you want to do. Do you need to find a mentor or someone to help you learn a new task? This is the time to research where those people gather. Find out what organizations or social groups they belong to and join them.

For those relationships that you want to grow and nurture, first you need to discover where you are in the relationship and what changes need to be made. A great question to ask the other person to find out that information is: "On a scale of one to ten, how would you rate the quality of our relationship?" If the person's answer is any number less than ten, follow up with the question, "What can I do to make it ten?" These two simple questions allow you to establish the current quality of the relationship and give you the action steps you need to go ahead and improve the relationship. It takes away all of the guesswork. People tell you what's important to them. All you have to do is listen. And when you're listening, listen without distraction. Turn off cell phones, TVs, or computers and focus on what is being said.

You should also seek completion with those people with whom you need closure. There may be some messes that you created that need to be cleaned up. Go get the broom and go to work! Is there someone in your life to whom you owe an apology? Is there someone who you feel owes you an apology, and you have been reluctant to address it? Are you harboring resentment over a past hurt that you have not acknowledged? Are you looking for recognition from a significant person in your life? This is the time to speak up and let them know how you feel. You cannot move forward in creating the new relationships you need to push you closer to your goals until you have gotten closure on those that are causing anxiety and unrest in your life.

Success is all about relationships. Make the most of yours.

Chapter 13

STAY CONNECTED

Wherever the art of Medicine is loved, there is also a love of Humanity.

—Hippocrates

I'm done with treatment. Am I done with my doctor?

Absolutely not! Finishing your cancer treatment is a cause for celebration. But you won't be getting rid of your cancer doctors in that celebration. You must stay connected. Don't worry; you won't have to see the doctor as often as you did while you were getting treatment. But you will still see the doctor for follow-up visits. This may mean that you see multiple doctors. If you had surgery, you will see your surgeon. If you had chemotherapy, you will see your medical oncologist. And if you had radiation treatments, you will see your radiation oncologist, too.

I would suggest that you stagger your appointments so that you're seeing someone every couple of months. I would not try to see all three doctors during the same week, or even during the same month. I know this may seem like a lot, but the more doctors that are following you, the less likely it is that something will get missed.

Follow-up care with your cancer doctor is very important after finishing cancer treatment. There are many reasons why we follow you closely after finishing treatment:

- We look at the side effects that happened during your treatment and monitor them as they go away.

- If they don't go away, we give you things to help relieve or eliminate the symptoms.

- We watch for side effects that can show up months or even years after treatment has finished.

- We monitor you closely to see if the cancer comes back by ordering the appropriate tests and x-rays at the proper intervals and doing clinical exams to look for signs of recurrence.

- We assist you in finding ways and programs to help you regain strength, physical functioning, and independence that you may have lost due to cancer or its treatment.

- We assist you in making positive lifestyle changes that will help prevent your cancer from coming back and prevent you from getting a second cancer. This includes eating healthier foods, exercising more, stopping tobacco use, limiting the amount of alcohol you drink, and finding positive ways to manage stress.

Even though you're seeing the doctor on a regular basis, there are still things that you can do to help us monitor your health after treatment. Tell your doctor if you're having any unusual or abnormal symptoms such as pain, shortness of breath, or headaches that get worse or don't go away. Even if the complaint or problem seems trivial, if it does not go away or gets worse, then it needs to be evaluated. If your appointment with the doctor is not for several weeks or months, call the doctor's office to let them know that you're having problems and schedule an appointment to come in sooner. Also, let your doctor know when you start any new medications or stop any medications that you were previously on. When lab work or x-rays are ordered, make sure that you get them as scheduled. Make sure that you get the results of those labs or x-rays too. Don't assume that no news is good news. If you don't have an appointment scheduled to come back and get your results, then call the doctor's office to get your results if they don't call you.

Follow-up care is very important. Getting rid of the cancer is one thing, but making sure that it stays away or, if it does return, that you can start treatment right away is the ultimate goal. In addition to your cancer doctors, it is also important for you to continue to follow up with your primary care physician. Any non-cancer-related conditions such as hypertension, diabetes, colds, or the flu should be managed by your primary care doctor. It is important to get your yearly physical exams done as well. You should do all of your other cancer screening tests, including colonoscopies to check for colon cancer, Pap smears to check for cervical cancer, a PSA (prostate-specific antigen) screening to check for prostate cancer, etc. As the saying goes, an ounce of prevention is better than a pound of cure.

As far as prevention goes, there are potential health complications after having cancer that can be helped by foreknowledge and preparation. The flu, or seasonal influenza, is caused by influenza viruses, which infect the respiratory tract (i.e., the nose, throat, and lungs). The flu is much more serious than the common cold. The flu season typically runs from October to May. It is not known if having cancer increases your risk for getting the flu. But it is known that if you have cancer now or have had certain types of cancer in the past (such as lymphoma or leukemia), you are at high risk for complications from the flu, including hospitalization and death. Pneumonia, bronchitis, sinus infections, and ear infections are also examples of flu-related complications. Cancer patients and people who live with or care for cancer patients should not risk getting the flu. You should get a flu shot every year.

Practicing good dental hygiene by brushing and flossing your teeth twice a day is a must. Have your teeth professionally cleaned every six months. You should also have a comprehensive eye exam done every year as well. Certain cancer treatments can cause complications to the eyes that will not be recognized by your oncologist.

Living awesome after cancer requires that you be diligent in following the recommendations to prevent, limit, and diagnose problems before they make a significant negative impact on your life.

Chapter 14

MANAGE YOUR MOOD

Start by doing what's necessary; then do what's possible; and suddenly you are doing the impossible.

—**Author Unknown**

Sometimes thinking positive, setting goals, and repeating affirmations aren't enough to get you in the right frame of mind. Many cancer patients experience depression. It is estimated that greater than 10 percent of cancer patients suffer from depression at some point during the cancer journey.

Depression is a mood disorder. It can occur at any time during the cancer journey. Often times we see it at the beginning of the journey, but it is not unusual to see it as someone is finishing treatment. Being sad is a normal part of the cancer experience. It is expected that at some point during your cancer journey you will have some anxiety related to your future, finances, side effects, or body image. There is often disbelief, anger, or denial about being diagnosed with cancer. These feelings can be associated with trouble sleeping, increased or poor appetite, irritable mood, or trouble concentrating. These symptoms should not last more than a month. Support from family, friends, or a support group can help most people adapt fairly quickly. If these symptoms last longer than that, you may be suffering from depression. People who are depressed have a hard time coping with cancer treatment. They can also have difficulty making decisions. It is important to diagnose and treat depression, as it can also interfere with relationships and day-to-day activities and responsibilities. Here are some common signs of depression:

- Ongoing feelings of sadness and hopelessness for most of the day
- No interest or pleasure in anything
- Significant weight loss or weight gain

- Being agitated, pacing, or feeling like you need to move all the time.
- Moving slowly
- Extreme tiredness or loss of energy
- Sleep disturbances (too much or too little sleep)
- Trouble making decisions, focusing, or completing tasks
- Feelings of inappropriate guilt, worthlessness, or helplessness
- Frequent thoughts of death or suicide or making suicide plans or attempts

If you experience any of these symptoms that last for more than two weeks, you should inform your medical team right away. A suicide prevention hotline is available twenty-four hours a day. The phone number can be found in the list of resources in the back of the book.

Sometimes it is hard for your oncologist to differentiate true depressive symptoms from those that are related to side effects of your cancer or its treatment. Therefore, it is very important that you let your oncologist know of any symptoms, side effects, or concerns you have, not only those listed above. They can evaluate the true cause of your concerns and determine if they are treatment-related or due to an underlying depression. If you need medication, your oncologist can choose an antidepressant that not only treats depression, but can also treat other difficult symptoms that are interfering with your life.

After I completed my treatment and returned to work in my normal routine and schedule, I found myself very irritable. I was sad for no reason. I would start crying for no reason, without warning. I was really troubled that I was unable to control the feelings. I couldn't figure out why or what was causing it. My treatment was over and my life, I thought, was returning to normal. All I knew is that I wanted the feelings to stop. I talked to my oncologist and she suggested that I try an antidepressant. Although reluctant, I agreed to start taking the medication, in part because she told me it would also help with my hot flashes that began during my chemotherapy. After about three days of the medication, my mood lifted and I had a newfound euphoria. I felt a little weird at first. I now had a happiness that I couldn't control. The profuse sweating, warmth, and nausea that occurred several times a day was also gone. Thanks to my "happy pill" I was smiling and feeling better than I had felt in weeks.

After taking the medication for a couple of months, I decided to discontinue it on my own. Within a day or so, my anxiety and intermittent bouts of tears resurfaced. I restarted the medication and took it for a few more months. I ended up taking the medication for about six months before I was able to successfully discontinue the medication without rebounding back into my depression.

Treating depression in cancer patients is often complex and requires a combination of medication, counseling, and the learning of coping strategies. Cancer further complicates a life that is already complex. Many times there are additional life stressors that complicate your fragile state. This additional stress pushes our ability to cope past the point we are able to maintain control. Talking to a counselor or therapist is very helpful. They can help you identify emotional blocks or walls that you have up that are stopping you from being great. They can help shift your way of thinking and allow you to see the world through a different set of lenses. They can uncover personality traits and habits that have been keeping you stuck. Once the areas are identified, they can give you techniques and strategies to help you overcome the hurdles that once had a stranglehold on your life. They can show you how to cope more effectively.

If you feel you need to talk to someone, ask your oncologist, primary care doctor, or cancer nurse navigator to refer you to a licensed therapist who is experienced at working with cancer patients.

Don't get discouraged if you don't feel better right away. Healing takes time. Just like cancer treatment is a journey, treatment of depression is a journey as well. It can take months or even years to heal completely. Treating depression is an important part of getting to awesome. Without proper treatment, depression can interfere with the completion of tasks needed to get to your goal.

Chapter 15

PROTECT YOUR BODY

Take care of your body. It's the only place you have to live.

—Jim Rohn

Part of being awesome is being healthy. After being diagnosed with one cancer, you are at an increased risk for developing a second cancer. Since the vast majority of cancers are caused by lifestyle choices, it is important that you make the necessary lifestyle changes to reduce that risk as much as possible.

The National Cancer Institute says that smoking is the leading cause of cancer and death from cancer in the

United States. The American Cancer Society, in *Cancer Facts & Figures 2017*, estimates that smoking is responsible for about 155,000 cancer-related deaths each year. Those who use tobacco or who are regularly around tobacco smoke (secondhand smoke) are at increased risk of developing cancer. It is important that you quit smoking and limit your exposure to secondhand smoke. As a physician and survivor, it is disheartening to watch someone fight so hard to cure one cancer only to see them develop a second cancer because of continued tobacco use. Tobacco is linked not only to lung cancer, but also mouth and throat cancers and bladder cancers as well. This is the time to talk to your doctor about ways to stop smoking, using snuff, or chewing tobacco. Each state has a tobacco quit line. The number can be located in the list of resources in the back of the book.

Excessive alcohol consumption has been linked to mouth, throat, and esophageal cancers as well. Limit your alcohol consumption.

DO YOU KNOW YOUR STATUS?

Unprotected sex can lead to the transmission of human papilloma virus (HPV) and human immunodeficiency virus (HIV). These viruses have been linked to the development of cancers in the cervix, vulva, penis, anus, liver, lungs, skin, mouth, throat, and lymphatic system.

HIV weakens the body's immune system and reduces the body's ability to fight certain viral infections that can lead to cancer. Persons diagnosed with HIV have a higher risk of developing some cancers when compared to people of the same age who are not infected. HIV infection is also associated with an increased risk of dying from cancer. Treatment with highly active antiretroviral therapy or combination antiretroviral therapy has greatly reduced the frequency of certain cancers in these patients. It does this by partially restoring the body's immune system so it can fight the viruses that cause many of these cancers. Although it reduces the risk for certain cancers, it does not lower the risk back to the risk level of the general population, so it is important for people with HIV to pay close attention to their doctors and do the recommended cancer screenings they qualify for.

Human papilloma virus is the most common sexually transmitted infection in the United States. It is so common that almost everyone who is sexually active will get HPV at some point during their lifetime if they are not vaccinated. HPV represents a group of viruses, of which certain types can cause health problems. In many people, the body fights the virus and gets rid of it without treatment. In other people, especially in those with compromised immune systems, it can cause other health problems, such as genital warts or cancer.

You can reduce your risk of getting infected with HPV by using a latex condom and participating in a mutually monogamous relationship.

You can also reduce your risk of getting HPV by getting vaccinated as a preteen. All boys and girls eleven to twelve years of age should be vaccinated. Catch-up vaccines are recommended for boys through age twenty-one and girls through age twenty-six.

The Centers for Disease Control also recommends vaccination against HPV for women and men with compromised immune systems (which includes those living with HIV/AIDS) up to the age of twenty-six.

As of the writing of this book, there is no way to test a person's HPV status. Many people find out they have HPV only after being diagnosed with an HPV-related health condition.

Women should continue to get a routine cervical cancer screening up to age sixty-five. Many cervical cancers are related to HPV infection.

Chapter 16

SNATCH YOUR SEXY BACK

One should eat to live, not live to eat.

—**Ancient Proverb**

A body that is fit and healthy is a great fashion statement. And you want to look fashionably gorgeous, don't you? If you have lost a lot of weight, now is the time to try to regain that weight. If you have gained weight, now is the time to lose it. I've always told my patients to eat what you want while getting treatment. Cancer treatment is hard enough without the added stress of trying to follow some new diet. And many times there are only a few foods that we can taste or even tolerate while going through treatment. But now that treatment is over, it's time to start putting good things in your body.

It is really important that you maintain a healthy weight after cancer treatment. Being overweight puts people at increased risk for fourteen different types of cancers. The International Agency for Research on Cancer has identified that ovary, uterus, colon, rectum, pancreas, kidney, stomach, liver, gallbladder, thyroid, multiple myeloma, meningioma, esophageal, and post-menopausal breast cancer are all cancers associated with being overweight and obese. Maintaining a healthy body weight is the best way to reduce your risk.

Since the population in the United States has gotten heavier, many people don't realize they are overweight or obese. Being overweight has almost become the norm. The majority of people in the United States weigh more than what is recommended. The best way to determine if you are overweight or obese is to calculate your body mass index (BMI). The BMI is a calculation of a person's weight in kilograms divided by the square of the person's height in meters. Anyone with a body mass index greater than twenty-five is considered overweight. A BMI greater than thirty is considered obese. The Centers for Disease Control BMI calculator can be found in the list of resources in the back of the book.

Two years after I finished my treatment for breast cancer, I found myself fifty pounds overweight. Throughout my life I have always struggled with my weight. I have gained and lost the same twenty pounds at least five times in the last twenty years. But then I was twenty pounds heavier than I have ever been in my life. Even heavier than when I gave birth to my twin daughters, four years prior.

Carrying around all that extra weight made me feel miserable. After losing so much weight after my surgery and chemotherapy, I gave all of my larger size clothing away, vowing never to get that big again. Sadly, within six months of finishing my chemotherapy, my nice little flat tummy (from my tummy tuck that occurred as a result of my DIEP flap reconstruction) now created a muffin top on my sides.

On my forty-ninth birthday I made the decision that I would lose fifty pounds by my fiftieth birthday. I enlisted three of my good girlfriends to join my weight loss challenge with me so that we could encourage each other and hold each other accountable. I made small changes in my diet. I started off slow with exercise so that I would not overwhelm myself. With each pound that came off, my self-confidence grew. Not only was I boosting my self-esteem, I was also improving my health and decreasing my risk for a second cancer and other chronic diseases.

Changes in diet have the biggest impact on weight loss. Here are a few dietary modifications that can help you get yourself into a healthy weight range:

- Increase your consumption of fruits and vegetables.

- Limit your portion sizes and reduce the number of calories you eat.

- If you drink alcoholic beverages, limit your consumption to no more than two drinks per day for men and one drink per day for women. A drink is considered 4 oz. of wine, 1.5 oz. of 80 proof liquor, 1 oz. of 100 proof liquor, or 12 oz. of beer. If you do not currently drink alcohol, it is best not to start.

- Eliminate or significantly decrease your consumption of foods that are high in fat, low in fiber, and contain a lot of sugar. This includes most fast food takeout, processed foods, and desserts.

- Increase your consumption of high fiber foods, such as whole grains and beans.

- Reduce your consumption of foods that are high in saturated fats, such as red meat, pork, butter, and cheese.

- Eat fish that is high in omega-3 fatty acids, as it may have a protective effect. Animal studies have shown that omega-3 fatty acids found in fish may stop cancer from forming or slow its growth. The correlation in humans is unclear.

- Try to avoid consumption of processed meats or meats preserved using smoke or salt. These include deli lunchmeat, hot dogs, bacon, sausage, and canned meat. Consumption of processed meat has been linked to an increased risk of cancer in the stomach, colon, and rectal area. It is thought that this is due in part to nitrites contained in the meat.

It is not necessary to go vegetarian or even vegan to reduce your risk. There is no scientific evidence that following one of these extreme diets reduces your risk any further than making a few of the dietary modifications listed above does.

Losing even a small amount of weight will reduce your risk. This reduction is likely due to decreased levels of estrogen, androgens, and insulin that are linked to certain cancers. Getting to a healthy weight not only helps with cancer prevention, it also reduces the risk of heart disease and diabetes. Avoiding other chronic diseases also helps you be awesome after cancer.

Chapter 17

GET FIT FOR LIFE

*"Fitness is never really about what you lose;
it's about all that you gain."*

—Toni Sorenson

After completing treatment, many survivors find themselves severely deconditioned and out of shape. While getting cancer treatment, many of us are too tired to do much of anything. Cancer-related fatigue is a huge complaint experienced by most patients. This fatigue slows down even our normal activity. Many people who were getting regular exercise prior to cancer treatment have to stop because of the side effects from surgery, chemotherapy, and/or radiation. In addition, changes in your hormone levels from cancer treatment can cause an early menopause. This leads to weight gain. Medications such as steroids given with chemotherapy and the taste changes associated with chemotherapy or radiation can also cause unanticipated weight gain during treatment. This added weight slows us down and makes it harder to start or continue an exercise program. The inactivity leads to stiffness, further weight gain, and depression.

For years, health experts have told us of the benefits of exercise as part of a healthy lifestyle. After surviving cancer treatment, most of us want to do whatever we can do to stay healthy and decrease the likelihood of cancer coming back. There is now evidence to suggest that by exercising and keeping your weight at a healthy level, you can reduce the risk of cancer coming back. Adding exercise as part of your daily routine can also combat many of the ill effects related to cancer treatment. In addition, it plays an important part in helping you look and feel your best. Now that treatment is over and your energy is returning, it is time to slowly reintroduce exercise back into your daily routine.

Here is a list of nine more ways exercise helps cancer survivors:

- It improves your mood. Regular exercise is a great way to combat depression and anxiety and to improve sleep.

- It combats treatment-related fatigue. Regular exercise increases energy and decreases fatigue.

- It helps with weight loss and reduces weight gain.

- Exercise improves self-esteem and self-confidence. Some cancer treatments can cause changes in our body image that affect our confidence. Exercise can make you look better by toning your muscles and/or helping you lose weight and help you feel better about yourself.

- It increases lean muscle mass. This helps with long-term weight loss and body appearance.

- Strength training decreases lymphedema episodes and symptoms. You must have stable lymphedema before beginning any weight training. A well-fitting custom compression garment should be worn during all upper body exercises.

- It makes you stronger.

- It decreases joint aches in patients who use aromatase inhibitors. Combined aerobic exercise

- It improves bone mineral density, which decreases your risk for osteoporosis. As we get older, we lose bone mass, and medications such as aromatase inhibitors for breast cancer contribute to bone loss. The bone loss increases your risk of broken bones. Exercise counteracts this bone loss.

As you can see, exercise can quickly put you back on the road to better health and actually have you feeling better than you felt before your cancer treatment.

Here are a few ways you can add exercise back into your daily routine:

- Set a goal to walk at least ten thousand to fifteen thousand steps daily. Get those extra steps in by using the stairs or parking farther away from the door. The use of a pedometer, smart watch, or fitness app on your mobile phone can assist in helping you keep track of your daily steps.

- Do some type of physical activity for at least thirty minutes every day. This could mean taking a fitness class, taking a dance class, going out dancing, walking the dog, gardening, or even doing some household work.

- Join a walking club, run club, or other group fitness class. This will help keep you motivated and you will have others to hold you accountable to your fitness goals.

- Stretching, walking, bike riding, and yoga are all good ways to ease back into exercise.

Find something that is right for you. If your hands and feet are sore from the chemotherapy, you may have to find something that doesn't put extra weight on your feet and hands, like water aerobics or swimming. Some hospitals have return-to-wellness programs to help you get started. Ask your doctor or nurse navigator about it. Always, before starting any exercise routine, check with your doctor to find out if it is safe for you to start an exercise program. If you can, start slow and build up to at least 150 minutes of exercise per week. Work with a certified trainer or watch a video done by a trainer to make sure the exercises are being done with the correct form and technique. Doing the exercises incorrectly can cause injury or negatively impact your results.

Chapter 18

BE FULFILLED

The mystery of human existence lies not in just staying alive, but in finding something to live for.

—**Fyodor Dostoyevsky**

It is not possible to live an awesome life without finding meaningful work to do. To find meaningful work, you must discover your purpose. Do something that inspires you and challenges you to grow into a better person. Discover what you are passionate about. When you are doing something that you are passionate about, it doesn't feel like work.

Living with purpose makes life much more enjoyable. You have fun. It fights depression. It gives you something to focus on other than yourself. When you live with purpose, you are more focused and less likely to be distracted. Research has shown that living with purpose can create a psychological buffer against life's obstacles. You are more resilient and less likely to be affected by things that happen to you. You are able to find meaning in the things that happen in your life and thus remain content with your situation.

For years I knew something was missing, I just didn't know what it was. Although I enjoyed treating patients, I knew there was something else that I was supposed to do. Over the years I've tried doing many other activities outside of medicine, but none of them filled that empty space. Being diagnosed with cancer gave me the clarity that I needed.

After my surgery, I asked myself a question. If I died today, what legacy would I leave to the world? What positive contribution did I make to society? I realized that my purpose in life was not just to exist, but also to use my life experiences to create positive change.

As a physician and cancer survivor, I have the unique knowledge to transform lives both inside and outside the office. Cancer was a gift, given to me to help you. It was just my business until it became my diagnosis. When I personally experienced the challenges and obstacles cancer survivors face during the treatment journey, I discovered new ways to help survivors that had nothing to do with curing the disease. Now, helping cancer survivors transform their lives is my passion.

What is your passion? If you don't know what your passion is, ask yourself a question: What would I do if I had all the money I needed and I didn't have to work? Think about your hobbies and your interests. What things are you curious about? Ask your friends and family what you love to talk about. When you get the answers to these questions, you will have a pretty good idea about what drives you. Now take action. Try it out and see if you really like it. You will get clarity once you start doing rather than thinking about it. Once you identify your true passion, no one will have to push you or encourage you to do the work. You will have a natural drive and commitment to create all the success and fulfillment you desire. And you will enjoy every minute of it!

Chapter 19

FROM LACK TO LUXURY

I believe that through knowledge and discipline financial peace is possible for us—all of us.

—**Dave Ramsey**

I know you didn't plan to be off from work for three months or more; I didn't either. Hopefully you had enough sick days with your job, great disability insurance, and enough money socked away in an emergency fund that your home ran smoothly and you didn't skip a beat. If you didn't and were like me, keep reading. This chapter is for you. A big part of being awesome is achieving financial prosperity. To me, that means having enough money to live and fund your purpose without having to work.

As a self-employed physician, I thought that if I had three months' worth of money in the bank to cover my expenses, I would be okay. In addition, I had disability insurance to replace my lost income if I got sick. What I failed to realize was that my cancer treatment would take an entire year to complete and my disability insurance was sorely inadequate. It only replaced about 30 percent of my regular income. In addition, I didn't count on the extra expenses that come with cancer treatment, nor did I anticipate my husband losing his income during that time.

The cost of cancer treatment is very expensive, as is the cost of health insurance, if you are not being subsidized. A full course of treatment with surgery, chemotherapy, and radiation therapy can cost into the hundreds of thousands of dollars. Most insurance policies require the member to cover out-of-pocket expenses in the form of copayments and deductibles. These costs can run into the tens of thousands of dollars. Having health insurance doesn't make you immune to the overwhelming costs of health care.

Health insurance premiums in the United States are also very high; members pay anywhere from a few hundred to a few thousand dollars every month just to have insurance. Many people are struggling to keep their insurance premiums paid while all their other financial obligations are put on hold during their illness. When a person with little to no income is forced to cover these unexpected expenses, it can lead to financial disaster. A study from Harvard estimates that more than 60 percent of the bankruptcies filed in 2007 in the United States were a result of medical illness.

I accumulated over $175,000 worth of debt while I was going through treatment. I stopped answering the phone for fear of hearing a debt collector on the other end. My mail piled up as I refused to open bills that I knew I could not pay on time or at all. I had to go back to work part time during my treatment. There were days I went to work feeling sick, nauseated, and extremely tired. It wasn't the ideal situation, but it was necessary to keep my bills paid. I even consulted with a bankruptcy attorney after I completed treatment, only to be told that I wouldn't qualify since I had already restarted working full time.

Being unable to work and watching the bills pile up only add to the stress and anxiety you are already feeling about the disease. You feel powerless to do anything about it. Digging out of a hole that seems bottomless can seem impossible. But you can do something about it. It starts with making a solid plan to get out of debt and changing the way you deal with and think about money.

Your first priority is getting out of debt. In order to get out of debt, you must know exactly how much debt you have. Take an inventory of what bills need to be paid and find out exactly how much money you owe. Put your bills in the order of things with the highest interest rates first. The second thing you need to do is create a realistic household budget. Once you know how much you owe and how much money you need to cover your monthly expenses, you will know what surplus, if any, you have to pay down your debt with. Here are some tips to help you get out of debt:

- Start an emergency fund of at least $1000. This is important so that you don't have to borrow more if an emergency happens.

- Stop borrowing to cover expenses. This includes using credit cards or loans of any kind to cover expenses.

- Find ways to cut expenses. That extra money can be put toward your debt. Here are a few things that can be done to save money right now:

- » Stop shopping.
- » If you must shop because of large changes in weight or size due to treatment, use consignment shops or Goodwill.
- » Stop eating out.
- » Cook at home and pack meals to take to work or school.
- » Cancel nonessential monthly memberships to gyms, magazine subscriptions, satellite radio, etc.
- » Use coupons.
- » Buy in bulk—even though you buy large quantities, you purchase less often and it is much cheaper.
- » Review homeowners and car insurance policies and find less expensive policies.
- » Get rid of cable or downgrade to basic cable and/or consider lower cost options such as streaming services.
- » Look for less expensive childcare.

- » Refinance some of your higher-interest debt.
- » Consolidate student loans or defer payments if eligible.
- » Get rid of your house phone.
- » Find a cheaper cell phone plan.
- » If you use a lawn service, pest control, or a cleaning service, consider stopping them and have your spouse, friends, or family help out until your income recovers.
- » If you smoke or drink a lot of alcohol, this is a great time to cut back or, better yet, quit. These are very expensive and life-threatening habits.

- Find ways to make or bring in more money. Use this extra money to pay toward your debt. Here are a few suggestions:
  - » Find a second job. You can do some part-time consulting.
  - » Sell items you no longer want or need in a garage sale or on eBay, or consign some gently used clothing.

- » Return unworn clothing to the store for a refund. If you have clothes in your closet with the tags still on them, depending on when they were purchased and what store they were purchased from, they may still be eligible for a full refund.

- » Sell the extra car. If you have an extra vehicle that you rarely use, consider selling it. It will save on insurance and the extra money can be used to pay other bills.

- Put any extra money you get toward your debt. Things like tax refunds, rebate checks, insurance payoffs, etc. should be put toward your debt.

- Do not use retirement savings to pay off debt. If you are at that point, then it is time to consider bankruptcy.

- Pay off your highest-interest debt first.

Now, if you find that, even with doing all of these things, you are still making no headway on your debt, then it is time to consider some debt relief options. If your debt totals more than half your income, then bankruptcy can be a good option. Bankruptcy can get rid of any debt related to medical bills, credit cards, consumer loans, past-due rent and utility bills, and even some older tax debt. Talk to an attorney who specializes in bankruptcy to see if it is a good option for you.

Once you get your debt reduction plan in play, you need to examine your relationship with money. For most people, your illness just added additional debt on top of debt you already had. You need to change your money habits so that you don't end up back in the same situation again. Once you bounce back from this financial dip, you want to put yourself in a position to achieve financial prosperity.

Part of the goal setting you did in Chapter 5 should have included stating how much money you want to have and within what time frame. This should be calculated based on how much money you need for retirement, given the lifestyle you want to live and the charitable work and giving you want to do. Once you know how much you need, sit down with a qualified financial planner and create an action plan for accumulating the wealth you need. It is much easier to stick with your financial plan if you know what the end game is. Just saying "I want to be rich" is vague. When you know that you won't be able to live the lifestyle you want during your retirement if you don't generate the money that you planned for, you will be more focused on sticking with your plan.

Achieving your financial goals may mean creating a new relationship with money. You need to examine your personal relationship with money and where your attitude toward money came from. Was money a source of joy or a source of contention in your household? Were you taught to save a portion of your income or to spend everything that you had? Were your parents frugal about money or were they spendthrifts? Were you taught the importance of charitable giving? Poor money habits are often developed during our upbringing. Now is the time to develop new, positive habits around spending and managing money. Here are some great habits to adopt when dealing with money:

- Always put aside some of your income for yourself for the future. Do this before you pay any other expenses. This is best achieved by making it an automatic deduction from your paycheck. You don't miss money you never see. Save or invest this money so that you can reap the benefits of compound interest and watch this money grow.

- When making a purchase, ask yourself if the purchase is going to move you any closer to your goals and dreams. Is what you desire a true need or a want? And if you must purchase, use cash or your debit card. When you pay with cash you are less likely to overspend.

- Earn more money. This may mean learning new skills so that you can get a better job or starting a business and developing a new product or service.

- Create multiple streams of income. In addition to your primary job, there are many things you can do to bring in additional income to your household. If you work full time, start with things that require the least amount of additional time and energy. A few ideas include providing occasional consulting services in your field, creating an online business, and direct sales.

- Give at least 10 percent of your income to some type of charitable organization. It can be a church or other nonprofit organization. When you give more, you get more. The universe rewards those who give. In the Bible, Malachi 3:10 states that when you tithe, the windows of heaven will open and pour down for you a blessing that overflows.

Once you have created your debt elimination plan and adopted a new money mindset, you will be well on your way to achieving the financial abundance that will be an important part of your awesome future.

Chapter 20

CONCLUSION

Although cancer created this shift in your mindset, remember: cancer doesn't define you. Use cancer as the catalyst to push you toward your goals. Getting to awesome requires a 360 degree change. It requires a change in your mind, your body, and your soul.

All this change doesn't happen overnight. Be patient with the process. It took me one whole year to figure out what *awesome* was for me. It took another two years for me to figure out how to get there, and I'm still on my journey. My hope is that by writing this book, I can help you get there in much less time than it took me.

Set your goals. Break those goals into bite size pieces. Get into action and, before you know it, your life will be everything you ever dreamed it could be and more.

RESOURCES

The American Cancer Society: https://www.cancer.org

The National Cancer Institute: https://www.cancer.gov

Tobacco Quit Line: 800-QUIT-NOW (800-784-8669) All states have hotlines with counselors who are trained specifically to help smokers quit. Call this number to connect directly to your state's hotline. The hours of operation and services vary from state to state.

National Suicide Prevention Hotline: 1-800-273-8255 The Lifeline provides 24/7 free and confidential support for people in distress, prevention and crisis resources for you or your loved ones, and best practices for professionals.

Centers for Disease Control and Prevention: https://www.cdc.gov

Centers for Disease Control Body Mass Index calculator: https://www.cdc.gov/healthyweight/assessing/bmi/adult_bmi/english_bmi_calculator/bmi_calculator.html

The Beauty of Cancer Foundation: http://thebeautyofcancer.org

THANK YOU

From the bottom of my heart I want to thank you for purchasing and reading this book. I pray this book has been as much of a blessing for you in reading it as it has been for me in writing it. As a practicing oncologist, it is important for me to not only heal and treat disease, but also to educate patients in ways to create lives that are healthy, meaningful, and prosperous. As a fellow cancer survivor, I want to tell you that there is life after cancer. Cancer doesn't have to be the end; it can be a great beginning to a life you never dreamed was possible. Do the work and you will be amazed at the results.

I hope you enjoyed this book. I would love your feedback. Please let me know how I can continue to serve you. The tips for living an awesome life don't end here. I will be traveling all over the country talking to and inspiring survivors like you about how to live your best life now. Look out for my hands-on workshops and coaching that will help you get to the life you desire. I don't want you to miss a thing. Let's stay connected. Here's how:

WEBSITE:
www.DrTonyaMD.com

FACEBOOK:
www.facebook.com/DrTonyaMd.com

INSTAGRAM:
@DrTonyaMD

TWITTER:
@DrTonya MD

PINTEREST:
@DrTonyaMD

OTHER TITLES BY DR. TONYA

Mommy's Naughty Cancer
Dad's Naughty Cancer

Mommy's Naughty Cancer is a sweet and hopeful book that deals with a tough subject in a way that's easy for children to understand. Through dialogue and description, Dr. Tonya tells the story of a family dealing with—but not broken by—cancer, offering hope to anyone fighting the same battle. This book is perfect for families dealing with a cancer diagnosis of their own, and for anyone finding it difficult to explain what is happening to someone who has cancer. Children who read this book will not only walk away better informed, but will also have a sense of optimism and an understanding that cancer does not have to win.

Dr. Tonya is a board-certified radiation oncologist and cancer survivor who has treated many patients both before and after her diagnosis. She wrote this book to give others an easy-to-read and accessible description of cancer and cancer treatment so that no one has to suffer in the dark.

ABOUT THE AUTHOR

Dr. Tonya is a board-certified radiation oncologist and breast cancer survivor. She is also an award-winning author. When she was diagnosed with cancer, her twin daughters were only two years old, so she wrote *Mommy's Naughty Cancer* and *Dad's Naughty Cancer*, fully illustrated books explaining cancer to kids, which won the Indie Author Legacy Award for children's books. Her unique position of having treated and been treated for cancer has given her insight into both sides of the process that she shares on her blog, www.thebeautyofcancer.com, and her website, DrTonyaMD.com. Dr. Tonya continues to practice radiation oncology in the Atlanta area. She lives with her husband, Greg, her teenage son, and twin daughters.

CREATING DISTINCTIVE BOOKS WITH INTENTIONAL RESULTS

We're a collaborative group of creative masterminds with a mission to produce high-quality books to position you for monumental success in the marketplace.

Our professional team of writers, editors, designers, and marketing strategists work closely together to ensure that every detail of your book is a clear representation of the message in your writing.

Want to know more?
Write to us at info@publishyourgift.com
or call (888) 949-6228

Discover great books, exclusive offers, and more at
www.PublishYourGift.com

Connect with us on social media

@publishyourgift

www.ingramcontent.com/pod-product-compliance
Lightning Source LLC
Chambersburg PA
CBHW071523080526
44588CB00011B/1537